GEOGRAPHY

CAN BE FUN

MUNRO LEAF

J. B. LIPPINCOTT COMPANY

PHILADELPHIA AND NEW YORK

Before we start to learn about

GEOGRAPHY

I want you to meet

GEORGE

George lives in a place called Gettysburg where the people are always talking about NORTH and SOUTH.

George used to hear them talking and one day, a few years ago, when he was only about four years old, he asked his father what NORTH and SOUTH were.

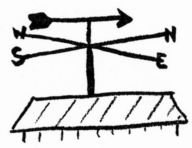

His father pointed one way and said that was NORTH.
Then he pointed the other way and said that was SOUTH.

George looked to where his father had just pointed, but he didn't see anything new or different and he said so. His father shook his head and said, "George, that's GEOGRAPHY, and you aren't big enough or old enough to understand it."

Even when he was only four years old that made George mad, and from that day to now, he has been asking questions and thinking and learning all he can about GEOGRAPHY—

This book tells you what George found out.

The first thing George found out was that he lived on the EARTH that is shaped like a big round ball.

It has air around it and spins through space like a top.

At first it was hard for George to believe that the EARTH is round, because it always looked flat to him, except where hills and mountains made it bumpy. It certainly didn't look round at all.

His father said that it didn't look round to George because he just couldn't get far enough away from the EARTH to see the whole thing. George *could* see that the SUN and the MOON are round, all right, because he was far, far away from them—millions of miles away.

Then George's father showed him a photograph of a part of the EARTH, taken by a camera that had been shot sixty miles up into space in a rocket. That picture of part of the EARTH looked like this.

So George said that if the rocket camera had gone still higher so it could *see* even more, he guessed it would have shown the whole round ball that we live on called the EARTH. AND THAT'S TRUE, IT WOULD.

What's more, George's Grandmother had once sailed all the way around the EARTH in a ship, and his Uncle Fred in the Air Force had flown all the way around it in an airplane. He had to stop for gas a few times.

Both of them though, had just kept on going in the same direction and after a while they came right back to where they had started from, because the EARTH really is round.

If it were flat, George's Grandmother would have dropped off and Uncle Fred would still be going.

But they didn't, so George said:

"All right, now I believe the EARTH is round, but how do we know that it spins?"

"That's easy to prove," his father said. "You know that it is light part of the time and dark part of the time, don't you?"

"Sure," said George, "it's light in the DAY TIME and dark in the NIGHT TIME—BUT I don't know WHY."

So his father told him that the SUN is a big round ball like the EARTH and it too is spinning around in space *millions* of miles away from the EARTH. It is burning like a big ball of fire that never goes out, and it gives off heat and light the way any fire does.

The heat and light from the SUN is what keeps our EARTH warm and gives us our light to see by in the DAY TIME.

"Why doesn't it give us light in the NIGHT TIME?" asked George.

"It is always giving light to some part of our round EARTH," said his father, "but only to the side of the

EARTH that is turned toward the SUN while we are spinning around. The part of the EARTH that is turned away from the SUN is in its own shadow, so it's always dark and cooler on the side of the EARTH that is turned away from the SUN.

"Every time the part of the EARTH we are on spins around so we can see the SUN again, that is the start of another DAY. When we keep on spinning around so we can't see the SUN any more and get to the shady side away from the SUN, that's when it grows dark on our part of the EARTH and we call it NIGHT TIME.

"ONCE every 24 hours we spin all the way around and we call one whole spin a

DAY and a NIGHT."

George said he could understand now about night and day, so his father said, "A little later on, I'll tell you why the part of the EARTH we are on is hotter in the Summer and colder in the Winter. Before we talk about that, though, let's see what you know about the

RULES OF NATURE."

George had found out a lot by asking questions about all kinds of things, and these are some of the most important rules he had learned to help him understand how and where people live on the EARTH.

FIRST

he found out that everything on our big round ball we call the Earth is either

ANIMAL or VEGETABLE or MINERAL.

The Animal and Vegetable things on EARTH are living and the Mineral things are not. George knew that he was living and his dog was living and the trees and plants in his yard were living, but the dirt and rocks and his pen-knife and bicycle were not.

He made three picture lists of different kinds of things on EARTH that he knew about. Why don't you make some like it?

ANIMAL LIFE

MEN DOGS WOMEN CATS BOYS MICE GIRLS

BUTTERFLIES FLIES BEES

BUGS RSES COWS SHEEP PIGS CHICKENS DUCKS

LIONS TIGERS DEER BEARS ELEPHANTS

SNAKES SNAILS LIZARDS WORMS

FISH TURTLES EELS LOBSTERS

VEGETABLE LIFE

TREES

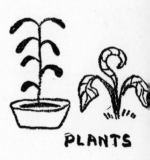

PLANTS

BUSHES

FLOWERS

GRASS

GRAIN

CORN

VEGETABLES

FRUITS + BERRIES

NUTS

COTTON

CACTUS

FERNS

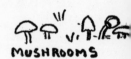

MUSHROOMS

12

MINERAL — THESE THINGS NEVER ARE ALIVE

ROCKS AND STONES   DIRT   SAND   WATER

METALS   LIKE   IRON - COPPER · TIN - SILVER · GOLD

...CIOUS STONES LIKE DIAMONDS - RUBIES - EMERALDS

ALL THESE ARE USED BY PEOPLE TO MAKE MANY THINGS

COAL —— AND —— OIL
ARE USED LIKE MINERALS BUT THEY ONCE WERE VEGETABLE OR ANIMAL.

PEOPLE HAVE LEARNED TO USE

ANIMAL - VEGETABLE - MINERAL

THINGS TO MAKE ALMOST EVERYTHING YOU AND I USE.

WOOD FROM A VEGETABLE TREE

STEEL SPRINGS NAILS SCREWS FROM MINERAL IRON

LEATHER FROM THE HIDE OF AN ANIMAL COW

ARE ALL PARTS OF GEORGE'S CHAIR. ——

The second Rule of Nature George learned is that All ANIMALS on EARTH have to eat other animal or vegetable things to keep on living themselves.

George found out that if there were no animal or vegetable life he certainly couldn't have any cereal or scrambled eggs for breakfast, or toast or milk, or bacon. And his father wouldn't have any coffee.

Do you know what each of those comes from?

What else do you eat?

All animals eat other animal things or they eat vegetable things of some sort. Cats eat meat or fish or drink milk from cows. Cows eat grass and corn and seeds from plants called grains. Fish eat other fish and bugs and vegetable plants that grow in the water. George and You and I and Pigs can eat almost anything—

ANIMAL or VEGETABLE

and we also have to have

WATER

to keep us alive like all the rest of the ANIMAL and VEGETABLE life in the world.

Trees and plants have to have

WATER

to stay alive just the way animals do.

So that was the third Rule of Nature that George learned:

LIVING THINGS NEED WATER

The fourth Rule of Nature that George learned was one he learned from WATER. If Water gets cold enough it becomes

SOLID

and instead of pouring like milk or gingerale or juices that we call LIQUIDS it becomes solid, cold little white flakes that look something like lace that we call SNOW
or hard round balls like marbles
or peas that we call

HAIL or SLEET

or cold, hard stuff that we call ICE.

After George
found out that
COLD
did funny things to
WATER,
his mother showed
him what
HEAT
can do to that same
WATER.

She put a lump of
SOLID ICE
in a pan
on the stove.
As it got hotter it
melted back to
LIQUID WATER
that you could pour.

When it grew hotter still and began to boil and bubble
some of the WATER started to change into tiny little drops
that were so small and light that they went up into the air
in little cloudy puffs that we call STEAM or WATER GAS.

Those puffs of tiny, light
drops of water that formed in the
shapes of little clouds over the
pan are made of the same thing
that the clouds you see
in the sky are made
of—WATER.

17

SKY clouds are just big puffs of drops of water with
each tiny drop so small and light that it can float in the air.
When it gets cool enough to stop being a GAS like STEAM
and goes back to being LIQUID WATER
it falls back on the EARTH again and we call it—

RAIN

George made believe that he was
a Rain-maker and held a cold lid
over the top of the pan to catch the
little STEAM clouds.

When the tiny drops cooled on the lid, the steam stopped
being a GAS and became a liquid again, so the drops of
water dropped down just like RAIN.

George's mother then told him that everything on the EARTH is

a SOLID or a LIQUID or a GAS

and almost everything on EARTH can be changed from SOLID to LIQUID or GAS and back again if we treat them the right way and get them HOT or COLD enough.

That is the fourth RULE OF NATURE George learned.

He has seen SOLID iron get so hot that it melted and poured like water. He has watched the SOLID paper and tobacco in his father's cigarette get so hot that most of it went into the air as SMOKE GAS. And he has seen a hot LIQUID chocolate sweet stuff cool off in a pan and become SOLID fudge. And This is *IM-PORTANT*: George found out that the water on the Earth is heated by the Sun, so it goes up into the sky and makes Clouds. Those CLOUDS move around and when they cool off—down comes the water as Rain or Snow.

It makes the land wet so vegetable life will grow and then runs off again into ponds, lakes, streams, rivers, seas and oceans. Then the sun heats it again and back it goes up into clouds and starts all over again.

Even without his father or mother helping him, George found out that everything on the Earth he had seen was either

HIGH   LOW

WET   OR   DRY

HOT   COLD

SEVEN RULES OF NATURE

1. EVERYTHING IS ANIMAL, VEGETABLE OR MINERAL.
2. ANIMALS NEED OTHER ANIMAL LIFE OR VEGETABLE LIFE TO LIVE.
3. ANIMAL AND VEGETABLE LIFE BOTH NEED WATER.
4. EVERYTHING IS SOLID, LIQUID OR GAS.
5. EVERYTHING IS HIGH OR LOW.
6. EVERYTHING IS WET OR DRY.
7. EVERYTHING IS HOT OR COLD.

Now George was ready to find out what the different parts of the EARTH were like and how and why people live there or don't live there.

And

THAT IS WHAT GEOGRAPHY REALLY IS.

In this book about George and the GEOGRAPHY that he learned, don't think that George had a chance to go to see all the places and people and things that he found out about. Nobody has the time to do that. The Earth is much too big for any of us to see it all.

But George and You and I can read about places and people and things that we don't see, and we can learn a lot about them. Other people have been there and they tell us about them in books and show us pictures of what they saw.

That is part of the fun of learning to read books.

The more you can read, the more places you can pretend to go to without leaving home. Then when you get a chance to go to a place where you have never been before, you can see for yourself whether it looks the way you thought it would.

George did go to a beach once and saw an OCEAN for the first time. It looked like an awful lot of water to George, so he asked his father how much of the EARTH was covered with water.

He was surprised when he found out that most of the EARTH has water on it. There is about three times as much WATER as there is LAND on the outside of this whole big ball we live on called the EARTH.

Most of the WATER is in the OCEANS, but a lot of it is in SEAS that are really smaller OCEANS, and in LAKES and PONDS and RIVERS and STREAMS, in springs and hollow places under the ground, and even in little puddles like the one in George's back yard when it has been raining.

The part of the EARTH that doesn't have WATER on it we call the

LAND

and that LAND, like everything else, can be
HIGH or LOW
WET or DRY
HOT or COLD

In the places where the land is highest we call those parts

MOUNTAINS or HILLS.

MOUNTAINS   HILLS

MOUNTAINS are higher than HILLS.

HILLS   VALLEY   HILLS   PLAINS

Where the LAND is LOWER and FLATTER we call those parts

PLAINS and VALLEYS.

PLAINS are just bigger and wider parts of the low land than the valleys are. Some wide flat plains that are up fairly high above the level of the sea are called

PLATEAUS.

MOUNTAINS   VALLEY   MOUNTAINS   PLATEAU   PLAINS   HILLS

Whether LAND is WET or DRY enough for ANIMAL and VEGETABLE life to grow there depends on how much

RAIN WATER

falls on it.

Parts of the LAND that don't get enough RAIN for plants and animals to live well there are called

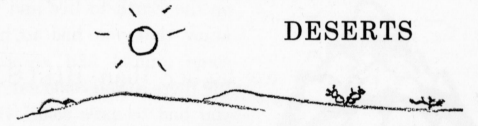

DESERTS

Some parts of the EARTH where it is warm and too much RAIN falls, are so thickly grown over with trees and plants and vines that men can hardly cut paths through them. Those places are called Jungles and they are often full of insects and snakes.

Other parts of the
EARTH are SO cold
all the time that
not much ANIMAL or
VEGETABLE life can
live there in the ice and snow.

All very high MOUNTAINS are too COLD at the top
for live things to grow. If you ever see a high, high moun-
tain, or a picture of one, you will see that there is nothing
up near the top but bare rock and ice and snow.

So if you had to find a place
on the Earth to live and you
knew that you had to have
some animal and vegetable
life there so you could eat, and
you had to have some water
too, WHERE WOULD YOU
PICK?

IF you were wise, you would look for a place
that wasn't too hot and dry like a Desert or too

hot and wet
like a Jungle
or too high
and cold so
that it was al-
ways covered
with ice and
snow.

If you look at a GLOBE that is a small copy of the EARTH, or at a WORLD MAP that is a picture of the parts of the EARTH, you will see where the biggest pieces of land are.

WE call those biggest pieces of land the

CONTINENTS

and George found out that they are called—

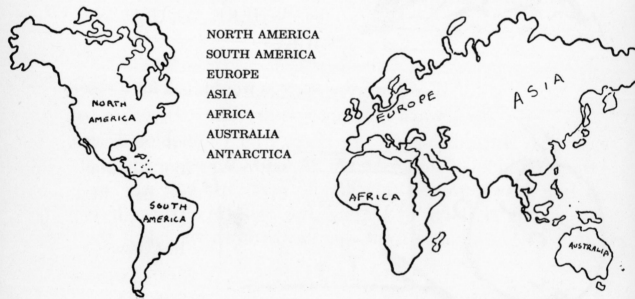

NORTH AMERICA
SOUTH AMERICA
EUROPE
ASIA
AFRICA
AUSTRALIA
ANTARCTICA

SEE IF YOU CAN FIND THEM ON A GLOBE.

How HOT or COLD any of these parts of the Earth's land are, depends on where they are on our big round spinning ball.

The coldest parts of the Earth are those near the top and the bottom. We call the place at the very tip of the top of the Earth the NORTH POLE and the one at the very tip of the bottom the SOUTH POLE.

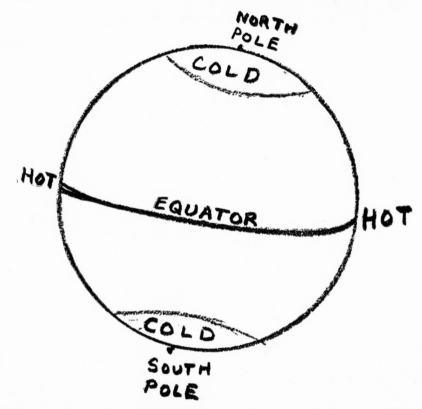

The hottest parts of the Earth's land are those near the fat middle of the ball. On all map globes you will see a line drawn around this middle part, just half way between the NORTH POLE and the SOUTH POLE. It is an EQUAL distance from each of them, so we call it the

EQUATOR

Can you guess why it is hot near the EQUATOR and cold near both the NORTH and SOUTH POLE?

27

George couldn't guess why, so his father told him and this is what he said: "While the Earth is turning all the way around once every day and night like a top

THE EARTH IS ALSO GOING AROUND THE SUN IN A BIG LOOP LIKE THIS—AND IT TAKES THE EARTH 365 DAYS AND NIGHTS—1 YEAR TO GO ALL THE WAY."

SUN

"The EARTH is always leaning a little as it goes on its path around the SUN,

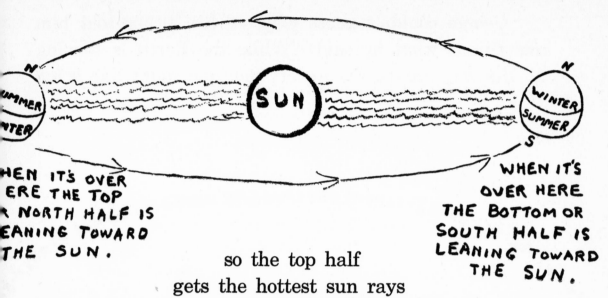

HEN IT'S OVER ERE THE TOP NORTH HALF IS EANING TOWARD THE SUN.

WHEN IT'S OVER HERE THE BOTTOM OR SOUTH HALF IS LEANING TOWARD THE SUN.

so the top half gets the hottest sun rays part of the year, and then the bottom half gets them. When the top half of the Earth that we live on is getting the hottest sun's rays we call that

SUMMER

"When the bottom half is getting those hot summer rays we in the top half are having

WINTER

and then we are colder. But the fat middle part of the Earth near the EQUATOR

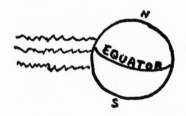

gets the hot summer sun rays all year."

If you want to know which way is NORTH from where you live, you can do what George did.

If you go outside at 12 o'clock noon on a sunny day and stand with your back to the Sun, you will be facing NORTH.

Straight behind you will be SOUTH.

Then if you stretch your arms out straight from your sides—

Your right arm will point EAST where you see the SUN first in the morning

and

Your left arm will point WEST where you see the Sun last at the end of a day.

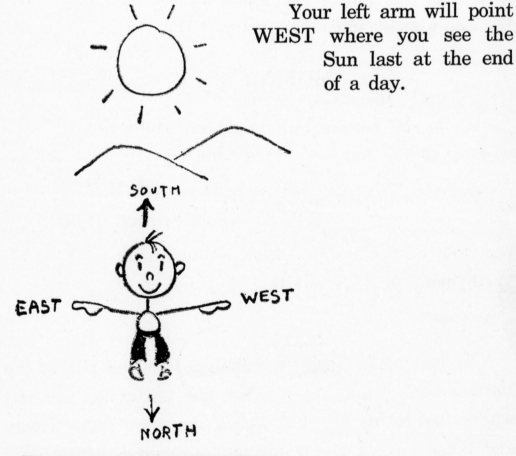

THIS ONLY WORKS AT NOON.

George lives in the United States on the CONTINENT of NORTH AMERICA and you probably do too.

So we will take a look at
George's Map PICTURE of the CONTINENT of

NORTH AMERICA

and see if there are many good places for people to live on it. Remember we are looking for places where it isn't

TOO HOT

or too COLD

or too WET

or too DRY

or too HIGH

or too LOW

for Animal and Vegetable life to grow.

By looking at George's map picture of this part of the Earth's land you can see where the mountains are and where the plains are and where there are many rivers and lakes to hold the water that all living things need.

The United States are not too close to the EQUATOR where it is HOT all the year—nor are they too close to the NORTH POLE where it is too COLD all the year.

They are in between, so it is just HOT enough part of the time and COLD enough part of the time. That makes it a very good PIECE of the EARTH'S LAND to live on.

Now, you could find a place that was just right for Hot and Cold and Wet or Dry, or High or Low, BUT you still couldn't live there if there were no good SOIL or DIRT for vegetable things to grow in.

Well, the people living in the United States are some of the luckiest people on the Whole Earth BECAUSE

much of the SOIL in North America is very rich and fertile, and that means that it is very good for raising Vegetable life. Trees and grass and plants of all sorts grow well in many parts of our country.

And if Vegetable life can grow well in a place,
then ANIMAL LIFE can grow there too, because it can get the other VEGETABLE or ANIMAL things it needs to eat and stay alive.

If a man has enough water and good soil, he can raise corn to feed cows and sheep, then the man can eat corn flakes and corn bread with milk and eat beef steak and lamb chops and he can wear leather jackets and wool suits.

MEN and WOMEN and BOYS and GIRLS are
different from all other ANIMAL LIFE.
They can THINK better and figure out
how to make things and USE TOOLS

WITH the TOOLS they make, people can use the other
ANIMAL and VEGETABLE and MINERAL things of the
EARTH to make living better for themselves and others.

Smart, THINKING people living on parts of the
EARTH that have MINERALS in them like iron, copper,
aluminum and lead, and with fuel to burn, like coal and
oil—

CAN USE THOSE MINERALS TO MAKE
MANY THINGS THAT HELP ALL OF US TO
HAVE EASIER AND PLEASANTER LIVES.

The land of North America that George and You and
I live on has a lot of the world's MINERALS in it, and the
people who live here have learned to use them in thousands
of different ways.

When the first white men came to the Continent of NORTH AMERICA, they came from the Continent of EUROPE. They sailed across the

ATLANTIC OCEAN

and when they landed here they found Red Skinned men they called INDIANS living on this big piece of good land.

There were only about 1 million Indians on the whole continent. Now there are more than 150 million people living in the United States part of North America.

Like many people still living in other parts of the world today, the Indians didn't know much about minerals and machinery. They did know how to raise corn and potatoes and other vegetables though.

There were so many wild birds and animals and fish here that the Indians, who had some simple tools like
Stone knives and hatchets
and bows and arrows
and fishing hooks and spears
could feed and clothe themselves and make shelters to keep the rain and snow off them. Shelter is a place to live in, like a tent or hut or a house.

FOOD   CLOTHING   and   SHELTER   are
what all people need
all over the whole EARTH.

At first the white men who came to North America lived on the land near the Atlantic Ocean where there were plenty of fish and wild animals to eat. The soil was good, so they planted crops and raised cows and pigs and sheep.

Year after year more and more white people came from Europe, and after a while they brought some Negroes or dark skinned people from the continent of AFRICA. As some of them moved farther West, they kept on finding good land to raise animal and vegetable life and they found all the minerals they needed to make tools and machines to help them.

They didn't stop spreading out to the West until they reached the largest ocean on the EARTH—the PACIFIC OCEAN.

They all learned to speak the same language

ENGLISH

which is what YOU are reading in this book. They learned how to do different things well and helped each other, so that no one family had to raise all its own food or clothing or build its own shelter.

Let's pretend to go with George to look at the whole United States to see how people live there and use the land and things that are

ANIMAL   VEGETABLE   MINERAL

for

FOOD   CLOTHING   SHELTER

(Maybe you had better bring along an animal-vegetable sandwich. It will be a long trip.)

George started looking in the town of Gettysburg in the State of Pennsylvania, because that is where he lives.

Gettysburg and all of Pennsylvania has a good climate. It is warm in the summer and most of the soil is good, so things grow well there.

It is cold enough in the winter to keep people from growing lazy the way they might if it were hot summer all the year.

Enough rain and snow fall in Pennsylvania to fill the lakes, ponds, streams and rivers and to make the ground wet enough for vegetable life to grow. There is good water for people and animals to drink, and enough to use in the factories where things are made.

Hardly any of this state is too high or too low to live on and there are good roads, railroads and airports, so people and products can be moved from one part to another very well. Part of Pennsylvania is next to the Atlantic Ocean so ships can stop there and carry things easily to and from other states and countries.

George found out that most of the grown people in his town work with machinery to make things to sell, or help those who do make things, in many different ways.

If you live in a town or city in the United States you will find many people where you live doing the same things that the people in Gettysburg do.

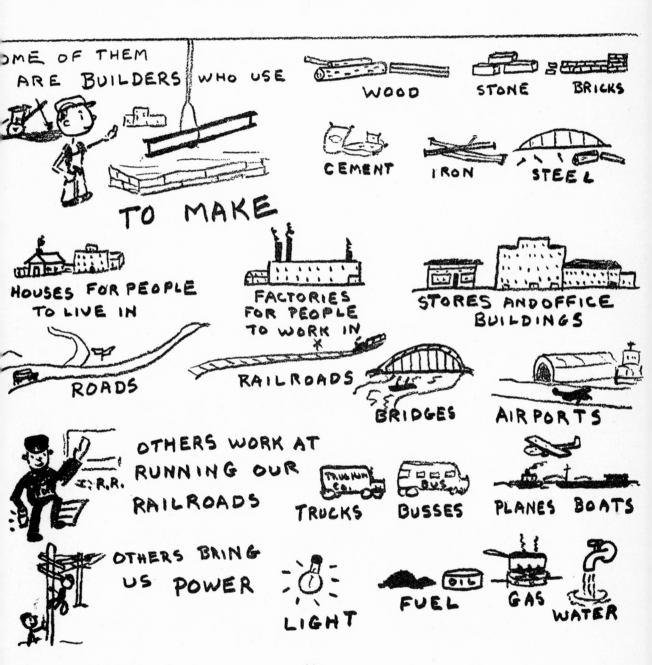

SOME OF THEM ARE BUILDERS WHO USE

WOOD   STONE   BRICKS

CEMENT   IRON   STEEL

TO MAKE

HOUSES FOR PEOPLE TO LIVE IN

FACTORIES FOR PEOPLE TO WORK IN

STORES AND OFFICE BUILDINGS

ROADS   RAILROADS   BRIDGES   AIRPORTS

OTHERS WORK AT RUNNING OUR RAILROADS   TRUCKS   BUSSES   PLANES BOATS

OTHERS BRING US POWER   LIGHT   FUEL   GAS   WATER

FIREMEN   **POLICEMEN**   **POSTMEN**   **TELEPHONE OPERATORS**

    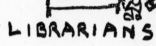

TEACHERS IN SCHOOLS AND COLLEGES   **LIBRARIANS**

DOCTORS   NURSES   DENTISTS   **RADIO   TELEVISION STAGE ACTORS**

STORE KEEPERS   CLERKS   TYPISTS   BUTCHERS   BAKERS   NEWSMEN

JUDGES   LAWYERS   BANKERS   OFFICIALS WHO HELP RUN OUR TOWNS, CITIES, STATES AND COUNTRY. GOVERNMENT

When we find a lot of people living and making things in the same place like a big city or a town like Gettysburg, we wonder WHY they picked that place.

The reasons are almost always the same, anywhere in the world:

1. The Climate is good—not too Hot or too Cold
                    and

2. There is enough water—for drinking and using in the making of things
                    and

3. The place is easy to get to over roads and railroads or in boats or waterways like oceans, lakes or rivers—
                    so

FOOD can be sent to the people easily
                    and

MATERIALS for them to use in making or manufacturing things can be sent to them easily.

Then

THAT IS WHERE YOU FIND THE TOWNS AND CITIES OF THE WORLD.

George's little town of Gettysburg has a good climate, good water, good food-raising land all around it and is easy to get to by roads and railroads.

The people there who work in the factories use machines to make furniture and textiles. Textiles are things like cloth and rugs and socks and stockings that are woven with threads of wool or cotton or silk or rayon.

WHAT DO PEOPLE MAKE
IN THE FACTORIES NEAR YOUR HOME?

PHILADELPHIA

is the biggest city in Pennsylvania and the third biggest
in the whole United States. It has good roads and railroads and is on the Delaware River so ships can go down
it to the Atlantic Ocean.

People in Philadelphia make:

Textiles—silk goods, hosiery and knit goods, woolens,
worsteds and cotton goods, rugs and carpets, ships, loco-
motives, tools, streetcars, batteries, radio and television
sets, books and magazines.

PITTSBURGH

is the second biggest city in Pennsylvania and the twelfth
biggest in the U. S. It has good roads and railroads and
is by the Ohio River and boats and barges can go from
there all the way to the ocean. Pittsburgh is close to land
that has some of the best minerals and fuels in the world.

So people in Pittsburgh make:

Steel, iron, coal and oil products, brass and glass, meat
products, bakery products, tobacco, pipe, cordage, paint,
varnishes, electrical machinery.

On the next page are the names of ten other big cities
in the United States, where they are, and what the people
make there.

New York City in
New York State on
Hudson River by
Atlantic Ocean

Biggest city in U. S. and greatest shipping center and busine
center. People make garments, millinery, lace, fur good
men's clothes, coffee, spices, bakery goods, small machiner

Chicago in
Illinois on
Chicago River and
Lake Michigan

Second biggest in U. S. and greatest railroad center in tl
world. People make meat products, iron, steel and oil product
candy, printing, clothing, machine shop and foundry product
electrical equipment, railroad cars and lumber product

Los Angeles in
California on
Pacific Ocean

Fourth biggest in U. S. People make rubber goods and tire
automobiles, oil products, moving pictures, furniture, dresse
meat products, canned fish, iron and steel products and the
process minerals—gold, silver, copper, magnesium, bora
granite, lime, cement, clay and gypsum.

Detroit in
Michigan on
Detroit River and
Lake Erie

Fifth biggest in U. S. People make three out of every fiv
automobiles in the world, airplane motors, aluminum, bronz
brass, machine tools, stoves, furnaces, paint, varnish, drug

Baltimore in
Maryland on
Patapsco River near
Chesapeake Bay

Sixth biggest in U. S. Great shipping center for coal an
grain. People make ships, iron and steel products, machiner
meat products, printing, chemicals, canned food, clothin
fertilizers, cigars, drugs and medicines, paper boxes, ston
clay and glass products.

Cleveland in
Ohio
on Lake Erie

Seventh biggest in U. S. People make iron and steel produc
from bolts to machines, motor vehicles and parts, paint, va
nish, oil products, electrical equipment, clothing, knitte
goods, chemicals, batteries, lamp bulbs.

St. Louis in
Missouri where
Missouri and Mississippi
Rivers meet

Eighth biggest in U. S. Largest raw fur center in the worl
People make grain and livestock products, shoes, drug
bricks, tile, stoves, enamelware, streetcars, bags, carpet
doors, chemicals, trunks, machinery and lumber products.

Washington in the
District of Columbia on
Potomac River

Ninth biggest in U. S. The Capital of our country where tl
Government departments are.

Boston in
Massachusetts by
the Atlantic Ocean

Tenth biggest in U. S. Wool trading center. Fish and Se
products, biggest shoe manufacture in the world, boot
leather goods, rubber goods, woolen and cotton garment
electrical equipment, ice cream and candy, meat packin
printing, machine shop products.

San Francisco in
California on
Pacific Ocean

Eleventh biggest in U. S. This is a great shipping center o
the Western U. S. Fruits, grains, minerals and oil are a
processed there.

When George found that more than half the people in the United States live in towns and cities, he wanted to know two things:

1. From where do they get their food?
2. From where do they get the materials they use to make things?

So he found out that most of the other people in the U. S. work on the land in one way or another

so

they can sell things to the people in the cities.

With the money they get the people who work on the land can buy things they want from the people who make things in cities.

A farmer that George knows, who lives near Gettysburg, sells milk from the cows he raises—and eggs that his chickens lay, and fresh vegetables that he raises in his fields—

to the people who work in Gettysburg.

With the money he gets, he has bought an automobile that was made in Detroit out of steel that was manufactured in Pittsburgh.

He bought a dress for his wife that was made in New York out of cotton that grew in the state of Georgia. He bought his son some shoes that were made in Boston out of the hide of a steer that lived in Texas but died in Missouri when they made beefsteak out of it. Somebody out in Oregon ate the beefsteak.

On Saturday night he takes his family to see moving pictures that were made in California, or they listen to a radio that was manufactured in Chicago.

48

A lot of us don't think about it very much, but most of the people who live in our country are better fed—have better clothes—and better houses than most of the people in any other country in the world.

The next time you squawk because you can't have an ice cream cone just then, remember that!

The names of our United States are:

Alabama	Maine	Ohio
Arizona	Maryland	Oklahoma
Arkansas	Massachusetts	Oregon
California	Michigan	Pennsylvania
Colorado	Minnesota	Rhode Island
Connecticut	Mississippi	South Carolina
Delaware	Missouri	South Dakota
Florida	Montana	Tennessee
Georgia	Nebraska	Texas
Idaho	Nevada	Utah
Illinois	New Hampshire	Vermont
Indiana	New Jersey	Virginia
Iowa	New Mexico	Washington
Kansas	New York	West Virginia
Kentucky	North Carolina	Wisconsin
Louisiana	North Dakota	Wyoming

If we divided our 48 states into five main parts of land we would see on the map that we have two big pieces of earth that are full of high mountains and hills, one in the East and a big one in the West.

Those high lands aren't very good places to have big cities, because they aren't easy to get to, and we can't plant big crops there very well,

BUT

luckily for us—they are full of minerals like iron, copper, zinc, lead, gold, silver, aluminum, and they have clay, stone, sand, coal, oil, gas and other things useful to us in making all sorts of things. Large forests of trees grow in parts of our high land too, and we get much of our wood from them.

Most of the people who live in our high lands work at mining and lumbering to get us many of the things we need for our Manufacturing in the cities.

George guessed that most of our people would live in the flatter land of our country where it is easier to raise food and to get from one place to another without having to go up and down high hills and mountains.

He was right. Almost all of our big cities are on the two parts of low fertile land that are near the Atlantic and Pacific Oceans and on the big, wide plains of rich growing land that stretch through the middle of our country between the Eastern and Western highlands.

Some of the best land in the world for raising corn, wheat, cotton, hay, oats, and different kinds of vegetables and fruits are in those three parts of our United States.

Outside the cities, in these three fertile parts of our country we find the farms and ranches where food and other useful plants are grown for us and for the animals that men raise, like cows, sheep, pigs, goats, horses and mules.

Out in the Western part of our big middle plain, the land is higher as it gets nearer to the Rocky Mountains. On the high plateaus of that part of our country, crops don't grow too well, and not many people live there, but there is enough rain and good soil for grass and small bushes to grow very well.

That is where people raise and take care of big herds of cattle and sheep that can get the food they need from the grass and plants that grow there.

All over the world you are likely to find people raising herds of cows or sheep or goats in the high or hilly country where grass grows well, but it would be hard to raise other big crops. Grass and trees will often grow on land that isn't good for farming.

Many people in the United States who live near the Atlantic and Pacific Oceans or by our Great Lakes make their living by catching fish and other sea foods for all of us to eat.

So George found that
most of the people in our country, who aren't busy in school or college learning how to make a living,
are

MANUFACTURING	FARMING
HERDING	MINING
LUMBERING	FISHING

OR

HELPING THOSE WHO DO THESE JOBS

And when George knew this, he decided to see what people do in other countries.

First he found out about Canada where our neighbors toward the North live. He went there once on a vacation and he was surprised to find out how much like us they are.

They do almost the same things we do to get their food, clothing and shelter from the land they live on.

Their piece of the Earth's land is bigger than ours. In fact it is the third biggest country in the world.

Only about as many people live there as live in our two states of Illinois and Indiana.

George wondered why that was so until he found out that much of the northern part of Canada, which is not very far from the North Pole, is so rocky and cold that not many kinds of vegetable life can grow there.

If it weren't for the great forests of evergreen trees that can grow there and the useful minerals in the land, the wild animals in the upper parts of Canada would probably never have to worry about many people bothering them at all.

In the southern parts of Canada, nearest to United States, the land is like ours and that is where most of the people live.

Near the Atlantic Ocean and along their biggest river, the St. Lawrence, they have good, fertile farmland for fruits, grain and vegetables, and Canadians are great fishermen. In their high lands they have good forests and valuable minerals and their great plains are some of the finest in the world for raising grain and cattle. They have plenty of water and the summers in the southern part are warm and good for growing.

Canadians manufacture more and more things, and they are making their country better to live in all the time.

Twice as many people live there now as did 50 years ago. They have twice as many railroads and they manufacture 1700 times as much to sell to people in other countries as they did then. You can see how fast they are growing.

While some of the people in Canada speak French, most of them speak English. The people from Europe who went to live there were mostly from England and English speaking countries like Scotland, or from France.

The people in Canada make their own laws and run their country the way they want to, but they also help in many ways a special group of countries called the British Commonwealth of Nations.

Those are countries in different parts of the world that the people of England once made the laws for, or still do today.

England itself is small but, because the people of England are good manufacturers and great sailors, they have sent their people to many different parts of the Earth's land for hundreds of years. Some of them stayed there and helped to raise things that could be sent back to England to be manufactured.

They have tried to make the countries where they settled better to live in, and many countries in the world now are parts of the British Commonwealth of Nations.

The main ones, along with Canada, are

UNITED KINGDOM (England, Scotland, Wales)	PRODUCTS: manufactured goods, textiles, machinery, cars, bikes
AUSTRALIA	meat, wool, vegetables, fruits
NEW ZEALAND	meat, wool, hides, butter, cheese
UNION OF SOUTH AFRICA	gold, diamonds, sugar, wool, hides
INDIA-PAKISTAN	cotton, tea, jute (used to make cord)
BURMA	rice, oil, wood
MALAYA	rubber, tin
THE ISLANDS of THE WEST INDIES	sugar, molasses, bananas and cacao

See if you can find them on a globe.

When George looked South from the United States to find out who our neighbors are, he found that the people of Mexico are our nearest ones. Still further South of Mexico he found a narrow strip of land, called Central America that joins North America to the whole big continent of South America and that stretches past the hot Equator clear down to the cold, icy seas near the South Pole.

People from all over the world have gone to live in the different countries south of us, and with the Indians who were there first they have learned to use their land in many ways.

Like the people who live on the other big Southern Continent of Africa across the Atlantic Ocean from South America, they have been busy mostly in raising animal and vegetable life to eat. Their minerals and other products that need to be manufactured have been sent mostly to Europe or North America. Mexico and most of the countries in Central and South America make their own laws, but almost all of the countries in Africa are run by governments in Europe.

The Continent of Europe, across the Atlantic Ocean from us, has people living on it who are very much like us and the Canadians.

George expected this to be so, because he knows that his own great-grandfather and great-grandmother came to the United States from Europe. Where did yours come from?

The Climate of most of Europe is pretty much like ours, with warm summers and cold winters. In most parts there is enough rain and there are lots of good waterways, roads and railroads so things can be moved easily.

Millions of people live there in towns and big cities, so, like us, they manufacture many things to use themselves and to sell to people all over the world.

Some of the countries have so many people in them that there isn't land enough for them to raise all the food they need. They trade some of their manufactured goods to other countries for the wheat or corn or meat and vegetables that they have to have.

The Europeans whose ways of living are most like ours live in the Western part in the countries of England, France, Germany, Italy, Norway, Sweden, Denmark, Holland, Belgium, Spain and Portugal.

They speak different languages from each other, but they all farm and herd and mine and manufacture on their land in much the same ways.

Because the people of Western Europe were good at making things and good at sailing ships, they sent people to all parts of the world looking for the products that they didn't have in their own countries.

They have been great traders and many of them have settled in parts of the world far away from their home lands.

The people of Eastern Europe are like us in many ways, but because they are closer to Asia and have mixed with so many different kinds of people for so many years, their customs and ways of living often seem strange to us until we know them well.

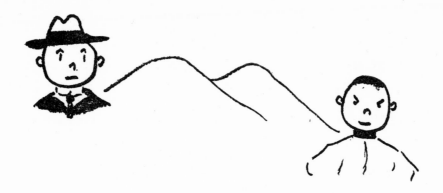

It really isn't very easy to tell just where the Continent of Europe stops and Asia begins, because they are separated only by the Ural Mountains that aren't very high.

The Ural Mountains are in the country of the Soviet Union which is partly in Europe but stretches clear across parts of Asia to the Pacific Ocean.

It has so many different kinds of land, high, low, hot, cold, wet and dry that the people of the Soviet Union use Animal, Vegetable, and Mineral products in almost every way that man has ever discovered.

Some live in big modern manufacturing cities and others live in tents as herders on their great plains, called steppes, just as their ancestors did hundreds of years ago.

The part of the world where people have to work the hardest just to stay alive is on the land of Asia. The big countries of China, India, Japan, and the smaller ones around them are so crowded in the parts where animal and vegetable life will grow that there is often not enough food for everyone.

Millions and millions of people live so close together that there isn't good land enough to live on unless they can learn new and better ways to use it.

Many people in Asia eat grains like rice and wheat, but very little meat, because it takes too much grain to feed animals to provide meat.

Nearly all the people of Asia are busy raising food to live on—not manufacturing for each other as we do.

When George learned that the Pacific Ocean is full of islands with one so big that it is the Continent of Australia and some are so small that only a few people live on them, he decided there was enough GEOGRAPHY to learn to keep him busy for as long as he wanted to know things.

There are the lovely islands of Hawaii that are a part of our United States, and our Alaska and Puerto Rico, and the many, many lands all over the EARTH with people living on them in many different ways.

When George had learned what is in this book, he felt that now he knew that—

Men, women, boys and girls
all over the world
are alike in some important ways.

They all have to have

FOOD   CLOTHING   SHELTER

and they have to get them from the

ANIMALS   VEGETABLES   MINERALS

of the

same EARTH.

George thinks it would be a lot happier world if all of us everywhere could somehow learn to help each other to use this EARTH

Wisely and Well

so we can all live on it as friends.

THEN

GEOGRAPHY CAN BE FUN